AR 3.2/0.5

What is Motion?

by Natalie Hyde

Crabtree Publishing Company

www.crabtreebooks.com

Author
Natalie Hyde

Publishing plan research and development
Reagan Miller

Editor
Reagan Miller

Proofreader
Kathy Middleton

Notes for adults
Reagan Miller

Design
Katherine Berti

Print coordinator
Margaret Amy Salter

Photo research
Katherine Berti
Reagan Miller
Crystal Sikkens

Prepress technicians and production coordinators
Katherine Berti
Ken Wright

Photographs
Digital Stock: page 7 (top)
iStockphoto: pages 13 (top right), 22 (left)
Shutterstock: Stefan Holm: page 4 (bottom); Natursports: pages 6, 24 (bottom); Foto011: page 17 (bottom)
Thinkstock: page 8 (left), 10 (bottom)
Other images by Shutterstock

Library and Archives Canada Cataloguing in Publication

Hyde, Natalie, 1963-, author
    What is motion? / Natalie Hyde.

(Motion close-up)
Includes index.
Issued in print and electronic formats.
ISBN 978-0-7787-0527-7 (bound).--ISBN 978-0-7787-0531-4 (pbk.).--
ISBN 978-1-4271-9016-1 (html).--ISBN 978-1-4271-9020-8 (pdf)

    1. Motion--Juvenile literature. I. Title.

QC133.5.H93 2014   j531'.11   C2014-900803-1
                                     C2014-900804-X

Library of Congress Cataloging-in-Publication Data

CIP available at the Library of Congress

Crabtree Publishing Company

www.crabtreebooks.com   1-800-387-7650

Printed in Canada/032014/BF20140212

Published in Canada
Crabtree Publishing
616 Welland Ave.
St. Catharines, Ontario
L2M 5V6

Published in the United States
Crabtree Publishing
PMB 59051
350 Fifth Avenue, 59th Floor
New York, New York 10118

Published in the United Kingdom
Crabtree Publishing
Maritime House
Basin Road North, Hove
BN41 1WR

Published in Australia
Crabtree Publishing
3 Charles Street
Coburg North
VIC 3058

Contents

What is motion?

Motion is movement. When something moves, it is in motion. There are things moving all around us. Fruit falls from trees. Balls bounce up and down. People run from one place to another.

There are many ways to describe motion. To describe is to use words to say what something is like. Sliding, jumping, spinning, and swinging are some words to describe motion.

From here to there

Motion is a change of **position**. An object changes position when it moves from one place to another. You change position when you walk from one room to another. Race cars change position when they move from the starting line to the finish line.

Objects can move in different ways. They can move in straight lines, zigzags, back and forth, or round and round.

Back and forth

Some objects move back and forth. First, they move in one direction and then they move in the opposite direction. A rocking chair moves back and forth when it rocks. Waves also move back and forth at the beach.

What do you think?

Which objects in this picture move back and forth?

Going in circles

Some objects move in a circle. This is called **circular** motion. Ferris wheels and merry-go-rounds are rides that move people in a circle.

Sort the objects shown below into two groups:

1. Things that move in a circular motion
2. Things that do not move in a circular motion

11

Zigzag

Some things move in a zigzag motion. They go from side to side. These skiers are moving in a zigzag motion as they ski down the hill.

A snake moves from side to side in a zigzag motion along the ground. These children are running through tires in a zigzag motion.

What is a force?

An object cannot start moving on its own. It needs a **force** to get it moving. A force is a push or a pull that creates motion. These marbles are not in motion until the girl pushes them with her finger. The push is the force that makes these marbles start to roll.

Even though we cannot see forces, they are at work all around us. In fact, without a force called **gravity** we would be floating through space! Gravity is a force that pulls things down to the ground. When you jump up in the air, gravity pulls you back down.

What is a push?

A push is a force that moves something away from you. The bigger the push, the farther the object moves. The boys use a small push to throw the ball a short distance. The girls need to use a bigger push to throw their ball farther.

Many sports use a push force. A hockey player pushes a puck across the ice with a stick. A soccer player pushes a soccer ball with his or her foot.

17

What is a pull?

A pull is a force that moves an object closer to you. You use a pulling force every day when you pick up a book or pull on a pair of pants. You are being pulled, too. Gravity pulls you down a slide.

What do you think?

Is this boy using a push or a pull to climb the rope? How do you know?

19

Contact!

Some forces touch an object to move it. They are called **contact** forces. This man pushes a lawnmower with his hands. His hands create the force that makes the lawnmower move.

Other forces make objects move without touching them. They are called **non-contact** forces. A magnet creates a force that pulls paperclips toward it without touching them.

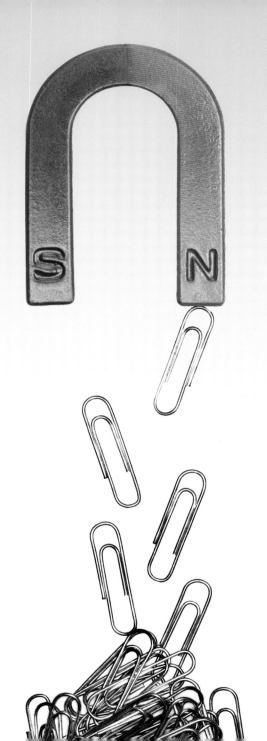

21

Move it!

The shape of an object affects how it moves. A ball has a round shape. A ball rolls when you push it. A book is a rectangle. It has flat sides. A book slides when you push it.

A rocking horse has a curved bottom. It rocks back and forth when you ride it. A sled has a flat bottom that makes it slide easily when it is pushed or pulled.

Words to know and Index

circular 10, 11

contact 20

force 14, 15, 16, 17, 18, 20, 21

gravity 15, 18

non-contact 21

position 6

Notes for adults and an activity
Activity:
1. As a group, brainstorm different physical activites that demonstrate motion concepts discussed in the book. **For example**:
Back and forth: curl into a ball and rock on your back
Circular Motion: holding hands with a friend and spinning around, using a hula hoop, etc.
Pushing Forces - pushing your feet against the ground when you run, skip, or jump
-A push-up (against a wall or the ground)
-We push a ball when we throw or kick it.
Pulling Forces -You pull on the monkey bars when you swing. You pull on a rope when you climb.
You can pull a friend on a wagon, etc.
2. Children can work in pairs or small groups to design an obstacle course that includes different kinds of motion and forces. You can create criteria that meets the needs of your children and the equipment you have available. Example course criteria:
-**Goal: Design an obstacle course that includes:**
-**One pulling force**
-**One pushing force**
-**A zigzag or circular motion**
-**Three different ways of moving (skipping, jumping, crawling, rolling, etc.)**
3. Each group must prepare a plan for their obstacle course that includes a picture showing how the course is set up and the different motion and forces used.
4. Groups will present their obstacle courses to others and identify the different motion and forces used throughout the course.
***Adults must supervise to ensure safety.**
Learning more
Books
Amazing Forces and Movement by Sally Hewitt,
    Crabtree Publishing, 2007.
Forces and Motion: The Best Start in Science by Clint Twist,
    Ticktock Books, 2009.
How does it move? by Bobbie Kalman, Crabtree Publishing Company, 2009.
Websites
This website includes an interactive activity that lets the effects of different forces
www.bbc.co.uk/schools/scienceclips/ages/6–7/forces–movement.shtml
This site provides several links to educational games that reinforce concepts related to motion and forces:
http://www.learninggamesforkids.com/motion-games.html

DISCARD